because...

To:_____

From:_____

I love you because...

I Love You Because...

Beverly Clark

I love you because

you
make me
laugh.

Love is friendship set on fire.

—Jeremy Taylor

In the arithmetic of love, one plus one equals everything, and two minus one equals nothing.

—Mignon McLaughlin

Love is the expansion of two natures in such fashion that each includes the other, each is enriched by the other.

—Felix Adler

I love you because

when I am strong
you are courageous.
When I am weak
you become nurturing.
I love you because
you can change as needed
between my warrior,
my mentor, my lover
and my friend.

—Patty De Dominic

Love is a taste of paradise.

—Sholom Aleichem

Love is like
a violin.
The music
may stop
now and then,
but the strings
remain forever.

They say in love
and marriage,
two shall
become one.
How I love
being one
with you.

I love you because

you are
my best
friend.

Love is much nicer to be in than an automobile accident, a tight girdle or a higher tax bracket.

—Judith Viorst

To love is
to admire with
the heart;
To admire is
to love with
the mind.

—Theophile Guatier

I love you because

in loving
you
I am
complete.

Love is like
chocolate,
too much
is not
enough.

To love someone
is to see
a miracle
invisible
to others.

—Francois Mauriac

When a woman
really loves
a man, he can
make her do
anything *she*
wants to do.

I love you because

you are
my
miracle.

Love is not
a union
merely between
two creatures -
It is a union
between
two spirits.

—Frederick W. Robertson

Approach love and cooking with reckless abandon.

—the Dalai Lama

I love you because

you let me
be me.

—Gale Wilson-Steele

What greater thing
is there for
two human souls
than to feel that
they are joined...
to strengthen each
other...to be at one
with each other.

—George Eliot

Love is like
a good wine,
it becomes
better with
time.

A wise lover
values not so
much the gift
of the lover
as the love
of the giver.

—Thomas À. Kempis

I love you because

you teach me
things
I never thought
I knew.

Love doesn't make the world go 'round. Love is what makes the ride worthwhile.

—Franklin P. Jones

You are thoughtful, kind, wonderful, adorable... face it, I have good taste.

Love is when
two souls
connect and
there is magic
in the air.

I love you because

no one
makes me
happier
than you.

Your words
are my food,
your breath
my wine. You
are everything
to me.

—Sarah Bernhardt

Love is always
bestowed as a gift -
freely, willingly,
and without
expectation....
We don't love
to be loved;
we love to love.

—Leo Buscaglia

I took one look
at you,
That's all I meant
to do,
And my heart
stood still.

—Lorenz Hart

You know it's love
when all you want
is that person
to be happy, even
if you're not part
of their happiness.

—Jean Zheng

I love you because

when we are
together there is
music and magic
and laughter
and love.

—Arlene Stepputat

Love does not
consist in gazing
at each other
but in looking
outward together
in the
same direction.

—Antoine de Saint-Éxupéry

Love is the
irresistible
desire to be
desired
irresistibly.

—Louis Ginsberg

One doesn't fall in love; one grows into love....

—Karl Menninger

I love you because

you are

so

cute!

Love is life
with
passion.

To keep your romance brimming with love...,
Whenever you're wrong, admit it;
Whenever you're right, shut up.

—Ogden Nash

Love is
hating
to be
apart.

The best
relationship is one
in which your love
for each other
exceeds your need
for each other.

—the Dalai Lama

I love you because

when something
wonderful happens,
I can't wait
to share it
with you.

In short
I will part
with anything
for you
but you.

—Lady Mary Worthly Montagu

Love is like
quicksilver
in the hand.
Leave the fingers
open and it stays.
Clutch it and
it darts away.

—Dorothy Parker

Commitment is something one grows into and then grows from.

I love you because

you are
you.

Photography Credits

A special thanks to the talented photographers who contributed to this book:

Becky & Erika Burgin, 831-688-2428,
www.artofemotion.com
Pages 36, 52, 71, 75, 80

G. Gregory Geiger & Caralee M. Kamens, 203-795-8651,
www.gregeiger.com
Pages 19, 44, 51, 68, 88

Stephanie Hogue Photography, 805-985-6022,
www.hoguephoto.com
Pages 3, 8, 47, 55, 59, 82, 92

Baron Erik Spafford, 805-569-9939,
www.baronspafford.com
Pages 11, 27, 35 ,43, 56, 64, 91

Richard & Lisa Scibird
Pages 76, 87

I Love You Because... Copyright ©2006 Beverly Clark
Published by Wilshire Publications
A Division of Beverly Clark Enterprises
800-888-6866
www.beverlyclark.com

ISBN-13: 978-0934-08127-6
ISBN-10: 0-934082-27-1

All rights reserved.   No part of this book may be reproduced or transmitted in any form or by any means, electronic or mechanical including photocopy, recording or by any information storage and retrieval system without permission in writing from the publisher.

Edited by: Cathy Feldman
Book Design and Production: Blue Point Books

Other Books by Beverly Clark:
Planning A Wedding To Remember
Fabulous Favors: Favors for Weddings, Parties, and Special Occasions
Heartfeld Thank Yous
All About Him
All About Her
Weddings: A Celebration

Printed in China

1 2 3 4 5 6 7 8 9 10

I love you